P9-AOY-190

Soul Winning Jesus Style

by Benjamin & Mercedes Williams

Teaching under the Prophetic Evangelism anointing

i

ISBN 0-9650644-0-9

Printed in the United States of America.

Unless otherwise noted, all Scripture references are from the King James Version of the Bible.

Graphics Designs by Mercedes Summers Williams / Wonderful Wonderful Accessories (Graphics & Publishing) 1-919-528-1739

Williams, Benjamin & Mercedes

Soul Winning Jesus Style / Benjamin & Mercedes Williams

TABLE OF CONTENTS

IN GRATITUDE

Many thanks to all who have stood with us in the production of this book.

Faith Community Fellowship Church, Inc., MS
Pastors Donald & Rosa Anderson
New Life Rock of Ages Christian Fellowship, MD
Pastors Benjamin & Eartha Butler
Eagles Summit Christian Fellowship Church, NC
Pastors James & Sandra Lilly
Life Giving Christian Church, NC
Pastor Aaron & Minister Carolyn Knight
Pentecostal Assembly of Jesus Christ, NC
Pastors Roy & Costella McKoy
New Destiny Christian Center Church, NC
Pastors Danny & Kymm Watson
Outlaw Carpet Service & Sales, NC
Edgar & Mary Outlaw
Delmar & Shirley Bradley Carmack, GA
Dr. Ruth Kennedy, NC
Larry & Bertha Richmond--Oxford Child Care, NC

Lorraine Maynard, NC	Johnny Holloway, NC
Grace Ukanwa Oke, TX	Theodora Moss, NC
Margie Peele, NC	Robert Blackwell, NC

Thanks for your generosity and support for the publication of this book. May the promises of God and the anointing of the Holy Spirit rest and abide with you forever. "The reward of the Lord shall be mighty upon your household, in Jesus Name, Amen". May God bless you richly and abundantly.

Pastors Benjamin & Mercedes Williams

FORWARD

"Soul Winning Jesus Style" is a much needed book that brings enlightenment to the subject of soul winning.

As Pastors of Benjamin & Mercedes Williams, we have witnessed personally the principles of this book in motion, in the lives and ministry of the authors.

You will be inspired and informed as you read the practical and spiritual truths of soul winning.

Prepare yourself for a new motivation and confidence in soul winning as you follow the guidelines of this powerful book, "Soul Winning Jesus Style".

Dr. Mack & Brenda Timberlake, Jr.
Senior Pastors
Christian Faith Center
Creedmoor, NC

INTRODUCTION

When the New Testament Church was born, soul winning was the major business of the Church. The Church was on fire with the Word of the Gospel.

They went from city to city, village to village, and house to house spreading the news about Jesus Christ, the crucified, buried and risen Lord.

Their powerful witness won them such names as "Christian", "disciples of the way" and "they which have turned the world upside down". What honourable names! These early Christians were saturated with Jesus. Jesus Christ was real to them every moment.

Can you imagine what this world would be like if it was saturated with Jesus instead of drug abuse, violence, illicit sex, and many other ills.

The need of the hour is for modern day Christians to evangelize a lost hurting world to Christ. It is time for Christians to come out of the closet and tell the wonderful story of redemption. We must rescue the perishing.

This is the message that is portrayed in this book presented by Benjamin & Mercedes Williams. They are two people who are well qualified to tell us how to win souls for Christ. They are soul winners indeed.

Dr. George A. Jones, Jr.
Former Pastor of Authors
Cross Lane, West Virginia

ACCLAMATIONS

Thank you for the opportunity to review your manuscript. "Soul Winning Jesus Style". Your book brings a refreshing approach to the often neglected art of soul-winning by articulating vital principles that many people in the body of Christ may not understand. Thank God for your obedience in publishing this book, and I believe that you will see the miraculous Hand of the Lord rest upon it as it shall stir up those that have been lax in their witnessing

Bishop E. Bernard Jordan
Zoe Ministries
New York, New York

Wise is he that winneth a soul. Very few people have the knowledge to win souls nor the skills to relate to people.

Evangelists Benjamin and Mercedes have written one of the most vital, well researched and practical approaches to soul winning that will illuminate the subject of soul winning, personal and group, and motivate the command to be a witness in Jerusalem and in all Judea, and in Samaria, and unto the uttermost parts of the earth.

I highly recommend this book. Read it, meditate on it, dissect it and digest it. Your effort to understand and act on the teaching in this book will enable you to maximize your potential as a witness for Jesus.

Dr. Jerry Kelly, Senior Pastor
Antioch Christian Center
Petersburg, Virginia

Proverbs 11:30 says: "The fruit of the righteous is a tree of life, and he who wins souls is wise." Ministers Benjamin & Mercedes Williams have tapped into one of deep secrets of the Kingdom of God that the body of Christ must manifest now! The Williams are on the cutting edge of what God is doing! Mastering "Soul Winning Jesus Style" should be a requirement for every local body of believers in Christ! We salute the Williams for their labor of love to unveil one of the many secrets of the Kingdom of God!

Pastors James and Sandra Lilly, Durham, NC
Eagle's Summit Christian Fellowship Church

"For God so loved the world that He gave his one and only Son, that whoever believes in him shall not perish but have eternal life."
John 3:16

God paid dearly with the life of His Son; the highest price He could pay. Jesus accepted our punishment, paid the price for our sins, and then offered us the new life that He had brought for us. When we share the gospel with others, our love must be like Jesus' -- willingly giving up our own comfort and security so that others might join in receiving God's love.

As we begin to love as Jesus loved, it often times places us in times of suffering and in positions of great sacrifice. Suffering can be a very difficult time to endure. Even though Jesus knew the reason he had to suffer and what type of suffering He had to endure, His strength came from His relationship with God. Jesus chose not to protect Himself from the pain of being separated from God and the injustice of the cross. He gave himself up to save others. When we give ourselves in service to Christ, we discover the real purpose of living; like Jesus, we die to ourselves, so that others might live.

With so many problems of our own, it is easy to lose sight of our primary purpose. Luke 19:10 says, "For the Son of Man came to seek and save the lost. Just as it is with Jesus, our first priority as believers is to save the lost." In the Book Soul Winning Jesus Style, Benjamin & Mercedes Williams have combined their unique gifts from God to win souls for Christ, and to train others in effective evangelism.

Bishop Eddie L. Long
Decatur, Georgia

DEDICATION

We give thanksgiving and praise unto Jesus Christ our Lord and Savior for being our provider and meeting our every need. **Praise the Lord, Praise God in His Sanctuary. Our thanks to the following love ones:**

Agnes Williams, Lagos, Nigeria mother of Benjamin Ademola Williams and Sarah Gorham of Beaufort, North Carolina, grandmother of Mercedes Summers Williams. Thank you mother and grandmother for always having faith in us. May God continue to bless and keep you. Our brothers and sisters of the Williams and Summers families, we love you.

All of the ministers of the Gospel who have invited us to minister to your church family, a special "God Bless You".

All our wonderful friends and acquaintances, so many, we can't name them all. Thank God you know we love you in the Lord. God bless you all.

Pastors, Dr. G. A. (George) & Ida Jones, Jr., our first real examples in the Gospel who worked with us seven years of our spirit filled Christian walk, we can't forget you. We especially appreciate you for understanding, releasing us to First Baptist, now CFC. Your support, as we moved to the second phase of our ministry training was appreciated. Thank you for continuing to intercede and stand with us. You are a blessing in our life with Christ. We challenge ministries birthed and developed under your teaching to get in touch with you.

Pastors Mack & Brenda Timberlake, Jr. and the CFC Family for allowing us to be a part of your ministry through volunteering, the Bible Institute since 1979 and full time employment 1990-1994. We will not forget the teaching. Hardly did we know we would serve as Deans, Secretary and Instructors from 1991-94. Thank you for extending full time employment as Associate Pastors from 1990-94, Directors of outreach ministries and other assigned duties.

Soul Winning Jesus Style

Soul Winning Jesus Style

CHAPTER ONE

"SOUL WINNING...JESUS STYLE"

Jesus Christ of Nazareth is the greatest soul winner of all times. He knows how to dismantle and disprove human philosophies, ideas, and wisdom. He knows how to introduce God's words and ways into the hearts of people. He has His own style; His style lends itself to success and successful living. In other words, Jesus has style.

All successful people have a particular style of doing things. Their style is what makes them unique; it is also what makes them successful. For example, a successful football coach must use certain techniques to train his team to win. A wrestler must train in a specific fashion to win a wrestling match.

A boxer must undergo certain training and preparation to win a boxing contest. Many athletes rise early in the morning, before many of us do, to train and to practice. They inconvenience themselves to be successful. They set goals, dream of achieving them, and dedicate themselves to being successful. In order to obtain their goals or dreams, they often put their personal conveniences aside.

TIMES & SEASONS

There are times and seasons that occur in our lives; ordained by God, as times in which we should achieve specific goals. God's timing is very important in achieving goals and dreams. God does not move in the lives of people according to our timetable. He sets the timetable in which we should move. In the Word of God, we can see where God uses "Seasons" to designate His timing. Man moves in days, weeks and years; God always moves in seasons. We see evidence of God's seasonal timing in:

Ecclesiastes 3:1

> **"To every thing there is a season, and a time to every purpose under the heaven."**

When you have obeyed God, His favor will begin to shine in your life. Because you have shunned the appearance of evil and have harkened unto the voice of the Lord, those who are without the camp will know. Your lifestyle will speak and move you into a season of blessings. The discipline you have incorporated in your life will launch you on the threshold of "delight in the law of the Lord".

Psalm 1:1-3

> **Blessed is the man that walketh not in the counsel of the ungodly nor standeth in the way of sinners nor sitteth in the seat of the scornful.**

> **But his delight is in the law of the Lord and in his law doth he meditate day and night.**

:3   And he shall be like a tree planted by the rivers of waters that bringeth forth his fruit in his season, his leaf also shall not whither and whatsoever he doeth shall prosper.

Jesus knows the perfect timing, for us, that the purposes of God be fulfilled in our lives. He knows that God's primary purpose for our life is soul winning.   He also understands the timing of life when it comes to this area of ministry. He knows when our soul winning season is ripe. He mentioned this to His disciples.

In Matthew 9:36-38, Jesus moves with compassion:

But   when   he   saw   the multitudes,   he   was   moved   with compassion   on   them,   because   they fainted, and were scattered abroad, as sheep having no shepherd. Then saith he unto his disciples, The harvest truly is plenteous, but the labourers are few; Pray ye therefore the Lord of the harvest,   that   he   will   send   forth labourers into his harvest.

4

Compassion is another key factor that Jesus uses in soul winning. Compassion refers to sympathy or sorrow that one feels for the suffering or troubled individual. Not only are we to feel their hurt, but it must accompany an urge to help or reach out to them: It is a serious type of thoughtfulness implanted in a deep love for the people of God. Jesus always moves with compassion towards our personal situations. Compassion, being embedded in love, encompasses charity. Jesus sees charity as an agent, instrument or an act of love. Love propels you to do things or deeds, in life, that you would not ordinarily do. It motivates you to help or aid someone who is in need of help or assistance. Love looks beyond the faces of people to see their needs, and propels us to make the decision to assist them. Charity is the actual act of kindness that compassion motivates and rejuvenates. It is, therefore, love in action. Both charity and compassion are essential components of a successful soul winning style. In other words, to be a success at the primary purpose that God has ordained in your life, you must train yourself to have compassion that manifests itself in charity. When is the best season for charity? Charity is always in season.

Remember in Matthew 9:36, that the people fainted and became scattered abroad. Even today, people all over the world are the same and in desperate need of the Lord. In numerous cities, homes, and communities they are crying out that they need the Lord in their spirit. Many teenagers especially do not know what to do or whom to ask. Some have no dreams, no purpose, no direction for the future as demonstrated by their lifestyles. All people need the Lord Jesus Christ in their lives for direction. His presence is necessary mainly because of what they are being confronted with on a daily basis. Crime, drugs, alcohol, sexual immorality, and the fear of what is to come have people, crying out for the Lord. Teens, as well as adults, are suffering from hopelessness. Jesus is our hope. Only He can fulfill this need, identifying our purpose in life and propelling us into the destiny designed by God from the beginning.

Wisdom Thought

"Some people act as if they have a thousand years before them, they spend their hours as though the store of them were inexhaustible.

CHAPTER TWO

"PRAYER LIFE...JESUS STYLE"

We will not begin looking towards the salvation of others, until our concern for their external lives and condition increases. The lives of people are important to God. Pray for discernment of spirits; many beg for help in their spirits. Because of past experiences, they are reluctant to share their feelings. They wait for us to move toward their infirmities. We should see them through the loving eyes of Jesus. All human beings face similar problems in life. They need to meet someone who will love them with the love of God; willing to admit, "I've been where you are in life, the Lord delivered me." Only the love of God addresses the vast variety of problems faced by many people today. They need salvation; and, they need us to reach out to them. Jesus encountered the same situations. He moved with compassion to meet the needs of the people. He showed them the love of God through His compassionate acts of charity.

Psalm 5:1-4 tells us:

> *"Give ear to my words, O LORD, consider my meditation. Hearken unto the voice of my cry, my King, and my God: for unto thee will I pray. My voice shalt thou hear in the morning, O LORD; in the morning will I direct my prayer unto thee, and will look up. For thou art not a God that hath pleasure in wickedness: neither shall evil dwell with thee."*

Remember Jesus tells us in Matthew 9:37-38: "The harvest is truly plenteous, but the laborers are few. Pray ye therefore the LORD of the harvest that HE will send forth laborers into HIS harvest."

Prayer is the key that opens heaven's door. As we pray for a situation, God can turn that situation around for His glory. Jesus Christ instructed us to pray just as He asked His disciples to pray. Our prayer is that God will send laborers into His harvest field.

Second Chronicles 7:14 states:

> **"If my people, which are called by my name, shall humble themselves, and pray, and seek my face, and turn from their wicked ways; then will I hear from heaven, and will forgive their sin, and will heal their land."**

When we pray, God listens and hears our prayers. Our prayer must line up with His Word and we must not have wrong motives. Praying in this manner guarantees that God will always grant our petitions. When we have the right motives, coupled with the desire to win the lost to Jesus Christ, we get God's special attention. We reveal concern for people and their needs; changing their destiny for the glory of God.

Psalm 2:7-8 indicates:

> **"I will declare the decree: the
> LORD hath said unto me, Thou art my
> Son; this day have I begotten thee. Ask
> of me, and I shall give thee the heathen
> for thine inheritance, and the uttermost
> parts of the earth for thy possession."**

The heathens are people who are not in covenant with the true and living God. Historically, these people did not worship the God of Israel. These irreligious and unenlightened people worship many gods. They were not proven children of God. They are the people whom God wants us to witness to and instruct in the ways of the Lord more perfectly. It does not matter where or who they are in life. All that matters is that there should be a covenant between them and God. They also have to have a relationship with Jesus. The commitment of serving God through our Lord and Savior Jesus Christ should be a lifestyle. God wants us to commit our lives to His only begotten Son, Jesus Christ, who came to save the lost.

FASTING AND PRAYER

A day before we go out to witness for the Lord, we need to fast and pray. We should seek God for His wisdom and understanding of how to minister to the people. This time must be a time of fasting and setting ourselves apart before God, not just a time in which we go about our daily hectic schedules without eating. We are trying to attain the mind of God. We will never achieve anything in life unless we accomplished it by the Spirit of God for His glory.

There are some communities or towns that need the joint fasting of two people. Other communities may require the collective fasting and prayer of an entire congregation. This fasting and praying must emanate so that the anointing destroys demonic activities and stops principalities assigned to those communities. Once this happens, those souls affected transfer to the authority Jesus Christ in the earth. We must immediately get them converted and trained. As Christians, we need to position

12

ourselves so that God can have His way in our lives. Our availability is also important to Him.

Jesus tells us, in His Word, about a boy that was demon possessed and had a dumb spirit. He made a statement that we should strongly consider before challenging a demonic force in another person's life.

Jesus said in Mark 9:29:

> ***"And he said unto them, This kind can come forth by nothing, but by prayer and fasting."***

There are areas where the demonic powers of drugs and alcohol are the controlling spirits in a community. They will refuse to leave that area without a fight. Through the power of the Holy Spirit, the anointing destroys that yoke; the anointing, acquired through fasting and prayer, is our only hope in destroying the work of the devil. In your ministry or in your personal life, some things will not come forth until you implement the principles of fasting and praying. "We are not

13

wrestling against flesh and blood but against principalities, against powers, against the rulers of the darkness of this world, and against spiritual wickedness in high places." (Ephesians 6:12)

In a wrestling match, there is physical combat. Both combatants want to win, and they both use everything at their disposal. They use everything that they possess to help them gain the advantage. Both parties involved have to come into combat physically ready and mentally alert, to protect themselves from being hurt. They also have to come emotionally prepared to do whatever it takes to win.

In the spiritual realm, our consecrated lifestyle in fasting and praying is our weapon against the evil forces. Our whole body, mind and spirit are wrestling against these forces. Through fasting and prayer, we keep Satan from destroying us in this battle. God Almighty completely protects the area for which we are fasting and praying. He honors these prayers; in return, He protects us and gives us wonderful results. The Christian wins the wrestling contest through spiritual training and readiness. God is good all the time. He wants His children to be the champions in these spiritual wrestling matches. We are the head and not the tail; above and not beneath.

Deuteronomy 28:13

> **"And the LORD shall make thee the head, and not the tail; and thou shalt be above only, and thou shalt not be beneath; if that thou hearken unto the commandments of the LORD thy God, which I command thee this day, to observe and to do them."**

When we spend time with the Lord in prayer, it elevates our level of joy and trust in Him. The joy of the Lord is our strength. This tells us that when we humble ourselves, pray and seek God's face, we become strong. Subsequently, when we stand firm on God's Word, we give great joy to the Lord. When we give such joy to Him, He strengthens us through our prayers and through His Word. Do you want to make God happy? Then, be strong in the Lord and in the power of His might.

Fasting helps to cleanse our minds as well as our bodies. It develops holiness in our personal life, fosters a wholesome relationship with the Father and increases our sensitivity to the voice of God. We become more sensitive to His voice, His ways, and His thoughts.

During our times of fasting, God begins to fill us with His knowledge, understanding, and wisdom. God gives us His wisdom liberally and with no strings attached.

Wisdom-Proverbs 2:5-6:

> **"Then shalt thou understand the fear of the LORD, and find the knowledge of God. For the LORD giveth wisdom: out of his mouth cometh knowledge and understanding."**

> **K**nowledge defined in **Webster's Dictionary as, "Denoting awareness; the act, fact, or state of knowing a range of information."**

When we spend time with the Lord in prayer, He will give us the range of information that will bless us or help us in our endeavors. He will give us a way to escape or conquer any situation that seems to overwhelm us. He will give us a way to remove the mountain from our viewpoint, that we may see His deliverance and find the peace that surpasses all understanding.

Wisdom defined in Webster's Dictionary as, "Denoting the quality of being wise; the power of judging rightly and following the soundest course of action; based on knowledge, experience, and understanding." We call It having good judgment or a wise plan; or course of action.

When we go out into the hedges and highways to win souls, we are to demonstrate and exercise good judgment when conversing with people.

17

We must employ and practice wisdom and judgment to minister to them at their own level. We must use knowledge and prudence to bring them to a level in God where they can have a good understanding of what He wants to happen in their lives. People are looking for answers. They are looking for a breakthrough. Many are seeking help in life; in handling their affairs. If we know how to minister to them as Jesus did to the woman at the well (John 4:7), then we can assist them or provide a source of relief for them. Once we show that we want to help or assist them, we will obtain favor and their confidence in what we say. After we achieve, prosper or succeed, we will earn their respect and get positive results every time we reach out. If we can attain a breakthrough in the spirit, then we can win souls for Jesus Christ our Lord.

*U*nderstanding defined in *Webster's dictionary as, "To gather or assume from what is heard; to know; to take for granted; to supply mentally an idea; grasp or perceive clearly; character." God wants us to understand one another in our everyday life. He wants us to know how to relate to one another without offending one another.*

Very few people really know how to relate to people, when it comes to soul winning. Jesus Christ knows exactly how to use wisdom in every situation, and through Him we learn to use the same wisdom.

Wisdom Thought
People who are truly successful are people who make the most of every situation. They know what they want, and are willing to go the extra mile.

19

CHAPTER THREE
"THE WISDOM OF JESUS CHRIST"

According to Proverbs 2:6-7

> *"For the LORD giveth wisdom: out of his mouth cometh knowledge and understanding. He layeth up sound wisdom for the righteous: he is a buckler to them that walk uprightly."*

Now that we have read this verse, we definitely know who gives wisdom. It comes from the Lord. We also know that knowledge and understanding come from Him. The Lord will give us a ready word to give to others as we grow in these areas. He understands the people that we are going to witness to more than we do or ever will. We must use common sense and courtesy when we go out to witness to people. When going out, demonstrate a genuine concern for their welfare and well-being. We must ask about their individual health concerns and their families as well. In our conversation with them, we should inform them of what we personally can do to positively impact their life or have people in place that can assist them. They want and need answers. We're the church, the body of Christ; we should have the answers. The world should be coming to us for answers. We have the living Christ, the chief cornerstone and guide, our shield and protector. "What can I do to help you or assist you with today?" Our tongues should be as a pen of a ready writer. These are just a few ways to get people to be open to us, in order that we have an opportunity to open the gospel to them. We want to witness to people without offending them concerning unnecessary things, and prying into their personal business without their permission.

People generally are nice, and are looking for "real people" in life to whom they can relate. They really desire to share with you what they encounter or go through. Most of them will not open up to you, if they do not feel that they can trust you. Often, obtaining the trust of a person may depend on their mood. Especially at these times, we must rely upon the wisdom of Jesus to get these people to open up to us. If we don't forget where we came from, we won't have a problem relating to them

Prepare To See His Wisdom

Now let us examine the scripture found in *John 4:7*. We see that there was a woman at a well with our Lord Jesus Christ.   Her concern about getting a drink of water opened a way for Jesus to minister to her.

John 4:7

> ***"There cometh a woman of Samaria to draw water: Jesus saith unto her, Give me to drink."***

Physical water is a naturally occurring liquid that forms as a drop, a river, lake, or even an ocean. The water that Jesus was asking for came from a well. The woman had to draw water up in a bucket to give to Jesus to quench His thirst.

John 4:9 states:

> ***"Then saith the woman of Samaria unto him, How is it that thou, being a Jew, askest drink of me, which am a woman of Samaria? for the Jews have no dealings with the Samaritans."***

At that particular time, there was racial discrimination between the Jews and the Samaritans. Mostly, they did not agree or do business together because of their racial and cultural differences. In this particular account, the woman was reminding Jesus that the Jews had no dealings with the Samaritans, because she could not understand what His motives were for asking her to give Him a drink.

John 4:10 states:

> ***"Jesus answered and said unto her, If thou knewest the gift of God, and who it is that saith to thee, Give me to drink; thou wouldest have asked of***

him, and he would have given thee living water."

Jesus begins to tell her of His motives. He really wanted to give her something. The Lord is always giving; just as He gave His life for you and me. He wanted to give this lady living water. We should offer the same living water to others. Present salvation to them in such a manner that its purpose will mean something to them. They may begin the conversation sharing their personal, mental, physical, or spiritual problems; these statements and concern open doors and avenues for witnessing. This is a perfect opportunity to remind them that there is always a solution for any of their problems through prayer. We can ask them if they have tried going to the Lord, in prayer, about their situations. Usually, most people love to have someone to pray for them or to stand in the gap for them even before their salvation. This is an open door for the gospel presentation. This is the perfect time to ask them about their eternal commitment. Don't just ask: "Do you know the Lord," but, "is Jesus Lord and Savior over your life?"

John 4:11 states:

> **"The woman saith unto him, Sir, thou hast nothing to draw with, and the well is deep: from whence then hast thou that living water?"**

The woman's interest was growing concerning this living water. Never had she heard such a statement about living water. She had always thought that real water was the natural water that she was drawing from the well. She knew nothing about living water, that water that has life in it. Streams, ponds, oceans, lakes, rivers, well waters are all different kinds of water. The woman was probably familiar with them all, but no one had ever mentioned anything to her about any living water. This both caught her by surprise, and captured her interest.

It would be very much the same for you or me today, if we had never heard of Jesus. If someone mentioned living water to you, you would probably be very curious. We would all be very curious. We would ask questions such as, "What kind of water is that?" What do you mean living water? We would begin to wonder about the differences between this living water and the water with which we are familiar. In communicating with people about Jesus Christ, our conversation is to be understandable. We do not want our conversation to be too deep. Our goal is to direct their thoughts to the areas that God would have us to discuss with them. We want them to understand exactly what we are saying, so that they will change their lifestyle to Jesus Christ's lifestyle.

Let us digress for just a moment. Great learners are not necessarily great thinkers. We want people to be great learners of the things of God, but it will seem very unnatural to them.

I Corinthians 1:26-27 states:

> **"For ye see your calling, brethren, how that not many wise men after the flesh, not many mighty, not many noble, are called: But God hath chosen the foolish things of the world to confound the wise; and God hath**

*chosen the weak things of the world to
confound the things which are mighty"*

Jesus has a way of describing things in a
completely different manner from anything we have
heard previously. People who are really walking
with God do not think, behave, or do other things
like people who do not know God. In their doings
and sayings you will find words of wisdom. That is
why people think that Christians are strange. They
simply do not understand. Why do Christians go to
church every Sunday or whenever the church is open
for service? Why do Christians relish the thought of
being different? These are deep discussions, and we
must be very careful about entering into such depths
with people who have only a natural understanding.

Getting back to our point, the woman at the
well stood, looking at Him in astonishment about
these living waters. This was something new to her.

In John 4:12, she asked:

*"Art thou greater than our
father Jacob, which gave us the well,*

27

and drank thereof himself, and his children, and his cattle?"

You can imagine the woman was saying in her heart, "Where did you get all of these great revelations?" In other words, she was asking Jesus if He was better than Jacob? Since they considered him as being the one who gave them the well, they were particular about him. The woman stated that all of Jacob's children and his cattle drank from the well. She looked astonished at the statement Jesus made that indicated He had something better to offer her. Generations saw that for many years the water from the well sustained the family. Now that Jesus mentioned the "living water" she was unable to visualize or understand the significance of what he was saying. She probably thought, "What kind of man is this talking about living water." "How could it be better than the water we are getting from Jacob's well?" She did not know He was speaking of the well of everlasting life.

When you minister to people about Jesus Christ, you are really giving them "living water." This water will change their lives forever. God is using you to show them the right path to their destiny. Previously, whether they knew it or not, they were working for the devil, but are now changing masters. Always make it clear that they will never go wrong by giving their life to the Lord. This change in status means no more bondage. It means being the head, not the tail and being above rather than beneath. They will walk with the "King of Kings," and "Lord or Lords, forever." God will raise them above whatever circumstances they are going through, and set them in Heavenly places with Christ. Where there seems to be no way, He will make a way for them. God will provide for them, and supply all their needs according to His riches in glory by Christ Jesus. Tell them that you know Jesus personally as your best friend, your big brother, your love, and your conductor in every area of your life.

WISDOM THOUGHT

"No conquest achieved without hard work. No conquest can give true pleasure if it has not required hard work and prayer."

CHAPTER FOUR

"A WELL OF WATER"

We have shared with you about "living water." Now let us look at another style of Jesus'. Jesus used more than one style, or pattern of thought, in winning the woman at the well. We should all adept or take on thought patterns like Jesus. His ways are higher than our ways, and His thoughts are definitely higher than our thoughts.

The Lord does things differently than we do in the natural. When we are thinking judgment the Lord may be thinking mercy, forgiveness, and love. Develop a habit and an attitude of thinking like Jesus. This achievement comes by staying in His Word, and by spending quality time in prayer.

During our personal prayer time, we can talk to the Lord about anything. When we go through life spending quality time with Him, we will always make the right decisions and be able to walk in love towards others.

The Lord always gives us opportunities to do the right thing or say the right things to His people to bring restoration in their lives. This is especially true if we know that their lifestyles are not in line with God's Word. Christians should not, and must stop, looking down on people who have not accepted Jesus Christ as their personal Savior in a negative manner. It is important that they be nurtured and won to Christ.

When an individual does not attend your church, or any churches you know, don't try to justify mistreating them nor do you have any right to judge them. God loves them, and can save them. He will deal with them concerning their commitment. Live a life before them that will draw them to the Christ in you. The Word of God says that we walk by faith and not by sight. The true salvation test is in the heart, not in the letter of the Word. Christians must

31

learn always to walk in an attitude of love towards those that are without the Body.

John 4:13 states:

> ***"Jesus answered and said unto her, Whosoever drinketh of this water shall thirst again."***

This means that natural water can never quench the eternal thirst of life. Nothing is wrong with drinking natural water. As a stated fact, doctors say it helps ones' internal system in many ways. It cools down the body and flushes impurities out of the body. It is essential in life sustaining processes. Pure water is better than anything that we can drink. In this verse, Jesus is saying to the woman that natural water will not quench your spiritual thirst.

John 4:14 states:

> ***"But whosoever drinketh of the water that I shall give him shall never thirst; but the water that I shall give him shall be in him a well of water springing up into everlasting life."***

Jesus introduced her to a new kind of water. He speaks of the water that He can give to us, by which we can quench our eternal thirst. Natural water temporarily satisfies this thirst, because we will always need to drink again to remain satisfied. The water that the Lord gives us is a well of water, in itself. It flows as a source of abundant supply springing up into everlasting life.

Whosoever shall call upon the name of the Lord receives salvation; and is delivered from bondage. The way in which we minister to people, about eternal life, means a lot to the Lord. Don't dwell on it; but don't forget from whence you came; once lost and doomed. Thank God, then remember those who need Him to deliver them. The Lord is holding us responsible for every life we come in contact with and have opportunity to influence. Find a space or an outlet where you can share the goodness of the Lord with them; He will open the door. We are to introduce them to the Lord.

People are looking for solutions to their problems. As you come in contact with people, share the love of the Lord with them. Do not waste any opportunity to share Jesus with another living soul. Tell them about JEHOVAH ADONAI - THE LORD JESUS CHRIST, our master -- the self existing one.

> **WISDOM THOUGHT**
>
> *"Find an outlet or a way in everyday discussion to share the Lord with someone. Be a blessing!!"*

CHAPTER FIVE

"GIVE ME THIS WATER"

John 4:15 states:

> **"The woman saith unto him, Sir, give me this water, that I thirst not, neither come hither to draw."**

This woman was immediately thirsty for the living and everlasting water. There is always a way to introduce the Word to people. They will be more hungry for the Lord if we use the right approach, the right method, and have the right attitude. Whether you acknowledge it or not, people are watching you. They talk behind closed doors about your actions, your deeds, and your conduct. Through you, they can make a decision to come to the Lord.

II Corinthians 3:2-3 states:

> *"Ye are our epistle written in our hearts, known and read of all men :3 Forasmuch as ye are manifestly declared to be the epistle of Christ ministered by us, written not with ink, but with the Spirit of the living God; not in tables of stone, but in fleshly tables of the heart."*

Here Paul introduces how we can be a living epistle of Christ on the earth. People can pattern their lives after us as we pattern our lives after our Master, Jesus Christ. Follow me as I follow Christ, our Lord. Many young people are looking for someone to pattern their lives after. They desire to have a mentor, in the flesh. Live a Godly life so that you can influence young people to go in the right direction. Let the life you live speak for you, in a positive way. It is an old saying, but it is true.

Our personal conduct always speaks louder than anything that we can say with our mouths. Always speak for and stand behind truth in your life. People will believe your words, because your words will carry life. They will see that Jesus is in what you say, and they will feel His Spirit. As you introduce people to the Lord, follow up with them. Call them or check on them. Give information to someone, that you trust, in order that they can assist you in follow up ministry. This will encourage them, and ensure that they do not give up on Christianity. Let your love shine forth towards them. Make sure that they know that you care. People can tell if you really care. People can tell if you are doing things for recognition or for vain glory. If people know that you care, you will always be a welcome sight to them. They will smile when they see you coming. They will welcome your presence.

The same is not true if they know that you are not sincere. They will greet you casually, and act as if your presence is unimportant. They will even try to ignore you. Knowing this, you will leave their presence immediately, and gain nothing for the purposes of God. Jesus Christ's representation would be inaccurate and the person's opportunity to receive salvation inadequate. Jesus is a real man with a real touch. He gives us, in His Word, directions for handling all situations. We must never neglect our responsibility to share the touch of Jesus. We must not allow our flesh to interfere with our mission for Christ.

Matthew 10:12-14 states:

> *"And when ye come into an house, salute it.*
>
> *:13 And if the house be worthy, let your peace come upon it: but if it be not worthy, let your peace return to you.*
>
> *:14 And whosoever shall not receive you, nor hear your words, when ye depart out of that house or city, shake off the dust of your feet."*

The Lord Jesus Christ is a wonderful coach. He provides us with wonderful plans. He possesses both a natural and a spiritual touch. He is human, and He is God. He is able to meet all the needs of all people. Many of those needs He will meet through us. We must never neglect our responsibility to share the touch of Jesus.

WISDOM THOUGHT

"Jesus is a coach with a Heavenly touch; meeting the needs of the people. He can feel us as we reach out to touch Him. He can feel our infirmities, and He can heal our infirmities."

CHAPTER SIX

"THE JOY OF THE LORD IS OUR STRENGTH"

WHAT MAKES GOD HAPPY

In the Old Testament, there were many things that God did not allow His people to do. This was because the law was their schoolmaster. However, in the New Testament we are under grace. Grace is unearned, undeserved favor. The children of Israel knew the acts of God. Moses was in constant fellowship with God; God taught Moses His ways. Moses passed these ways on to the people. Our obligation is to do the same for people of the world. Our lifestyle will be their mirror. We work and come in contact with them on a daily basis. It is a great way for them to learn of Jesus; learning by example. It is a continual process. It's really "on the job training". As we learn, we teach them, we will always be learning about Him until He returns. Jesus is still the same yesterday, today, and forever more. Jesus will always have something to offer to any man that will open his heart to Him.

John 10:9 states:

> *"I am the door: by me if any man enter in, he shall be saved, and shall go in and out, and find pasture."*

While in John 14:6, we find:

> *"Jesus saith unto him, I am the way, the truth, and the life: no man cometh unto the Father, but by me."*

The "way" in this scripture refers to the person of Jesus Christ. We have to learn of Him daily by accepting Him totally into our lives. We must allow Him to lead us into the green pastures of life. Only Jesus Christ can satisfy our soul and life. Allow Him to minister through you. Relax in Him, rest in Him, and meditate on His Word. He will show you great and mighty things of which you know not.

41

When we begin to win souls for the kingdom, it refreshes the heart of our Heavenly Father. Angels rejoice in Heaven, when even one soul comes to the Lord. If even the angels are rejoicing, what do you think our Heavenly Father feels. How much more do you think God loves His people, than do the angels. Salvation means a lot to the Lord.

In Psalm 20:5-6, we read:

> **"We will rejoice in thy salvation, and in the name of our God we will set up our banners: the LORD fulfill all thy petitions.**
>
> **:6 Now know I that the LORD saveth his anointed; he will hear him from his holy heaven with the saving strength of his right hand."**

When we see people coming to the Lord, it is a time of great rejoicing. They have found a new love, and it is the love of the Lord. They no longer belong to the devil. They now belong to a new master -- Jesus Christ. They now have a Savior. It's the

42

beginning of a new life. Many people don't believe that Christians should rejoice. They believe that Christians should look so pious as to appear sad. God rejoices over His people with singing. We should follow the example of God. We should follow His example in rejoicing over new souls.

Look at what Zephaniah 3:17 says:

> **"The LORD thy God in the midst of thee is mighty; he will save, he will rejoice over thee with joy; he will rest in his love, he will joy over thee with singing."**

Yes, when we see God saving people, we should begin to rejoice with them and over them. We know that God is happy and excited about their salvation. We should be just as happy. We should get excited that God now has His rightful place in their heart. God shows His joy, at them finding their way home, by singing and rejoicing. All of us should be of the same mind.

A MERRY HEART

Proverbs 17:22 states:

> *"A merry heart doeth good like a medicine: but a broken spirit drieth the bones."*

People with a good sense of humor tend to be more confident, creative, and emotionally stable. When you hear something funny, you should be able to laugh. If you don't, then you do yourself an injustice. The Word of God tells us that a merry heart does us as good like a medicine. Enzymes circulate into our system when we are happy or laughing, and these enzymes act even as pain killers. We're not endorsing careless jokes, or making fun of people in a negative way. We are referring to positive humor and amusement with genuine laughter. Listening to a good joke and laughing can greatly reduce stress. It will definitely make you a happier person.

We will discover, when we get to Heaven, that Heaven is a joyous place. It is a place of great laughter and singing. There is no sadness in Heaven.

Why can't we create such an atmosphere on earth? Let's laugh at the devil, and get him off our backs.

Humor does wonders for our attitudes and it is good for our health. Praising God also does good things for us physically, as well as, spiritually. Often, we do not realize how much praising God helps us to cast our cares upon Him. Praise draws us into God's presence, and brings total healing and deliverance to our circumstances. That is why we love and enjoy praising God.

WISDOM THOUGHT

A merry heart doeth good as a medicine.

CHAPTER SEVEN
"GOD LOVES A CHEERFUL GIVER"

When the Lord Jesus willingly gave His Life on Calvary, God raised Him again on the third day. By giving His own life for us, He gave us access to the tree of life. God is a good giver and He always gives His best for us. We have to develop the right attitude towards giving. We cannot just be a blessing to others by giving them salvation. Help them in any way that you can. We are not just to think about ourselves; we are to represent God by giving to others.

We also have to develop ourselves in the area of giving our time to the Lord. Spend time with Him in prayer, and give service to His people. Give favor to people that are not looking to receive back for favors that they have rendered to others. Give favor to those that cannot possibly return the

46

favor. Give your tithes and offerings unto the Lord, not unto man, or person, or organization. Though God uses man to accept our tithes and offerings, our hearts should release it unto the Lord.

Jesus speaking in Luke 6:38 said:

> **"Give, and it shall be given unto you; good measure, pressed down, and shaken together, and running over, shall men give into your bosom. For with the same measure that ye mete withal it shall be measured to you again."**

So, when we speak of giving, we simultaneously speak of receiving. Both of them work together. We also see that everything we have given out is going to come back to us in this lifetime.

II Corinthians 9:7 says:

> **"Every man according as he purposeth in his heart, so let him give; not grudgingly, or of necessity: for God loveth a cheerful giver."**

47

While it is good to give, don't do it under pressure. Don't do it, because other people are doing it. Don't give with reluctance. Give with a heart of joy, knowing that it will definitely come back to you.

The same principle involved in giving substance, is as giving your life to Jesus Christ. We should sell out completely to the Lord. We should give one hundred percent, not fifty percent. Dedicate and completely commit your spirit, soul, and body to the Lord. This demonstrates to God your will committed to Him. You will find new meaning and purpose in your life. God loves a cheerful giver, and you should love everything that God loves. Cheerfully give to God, and you will love the blessings you receive yourself. You will find that life has much more to offer you, because you have offered yourself to God.

WISDOM THOUGHT

"There are rare souls who have gathered their courage, faced the truth and turned away from a lifetime of achievement to answer a calling that brought them peace. They gave themselves back to Jesus; only Jesus Christ can satisfy your soul."

CHAPTER EIGHT

"PUT THE WORD OF GOD INTO YOUR HEART"

Many people have problems memorizing scriptures, or committing those scriptures to the tablets of their hearts. It is really very important that we familiarize ourselves with salvation scriptures, if we are to witness to the lost. At times we may cross the path of someone who is not a Christian, and they may even belong to some other religious group. They will not have a personal relationship with Jesus Christ. That is why it is very important for us to know the Word of God. If we are going out to win souls, one of us should know what the Scriptures have to say concerning salvation for the lost.

John 5:39 -- Jesus is speaking:

> ***"Search the scriptures; for in them ye think ye have eternal life: and they are they which testify of me."***

The Lord was instructing us that, through the Scriptures, we think we have eternal life. So at least have the knowledge of God's word, so that you can help the people that you will be ministering to. Failure to know the scriptures can adversely affect a person's whole life. A doctor or nurse must have knowledge of a particular drug or therapy to be able to use it to help a patient.

Remember also that it is the Holy Spirit that draws people unto you. If you are not familiar with the scriptures, then your own personal testimony can figuratively change people's lives. Your anointed testimony can be a blessing to the listener, because there is no one else that can tell it as you can.

WITNESS TESTIMONY

Revelation 12:11:

> **"And they overcame him by the blood of the Lamb, and by the word of their testimony; and they loved not their lives unto the death."**

Your testimony is the blueprint of your personal tribulation. You tell of how the Lord delivered you from trouble. Your testimony is a witness to the world that Jesus Christ is alive, and that He has overcome the world. It is okay if you do not remember scriptures like a preacher. Give your personal testimony as a witness for Jesus. Make it brief, but allow God to make full use of it.

The following is a list of ten points that you should remember concerning your testimony:

Things To Remember Concerning Your Testimony

1. Don't make it too dramatic, as it may put fear into the hearts of the very people that you are trying to witness to.

2. Make your testimony clear and straight to the point.

3. Let it proclaim, with clarity and conviction, that Jesus Christ is a healer and a deliverer.

4. Let it be edifying and comforting to the hearer.

5. Make sure that you focus all the attention on Jesus Christ. Although the Lord is using you, all the praise and glory belong to Him.

6.   In your testimony, don't give glory or credit to the devil by focusing on the problems. Focus on Jesus, the "Problem Solver".

7.   Speak as an over comer; do not speak as a defeated Christian. Speak with the power of the Holy Ghost.

8.   Be happy about the victory of your testimony.

9.   Be real in your testimony. Do not lie or exaggerate to make the Gospel look good. Be truthful. The Gospel is true.

10.   Let them know that you did not live saved all of your life; it will give them hope to trust in God.

Philippians 3:13-14:

"Brethren, I count not myself to have apprehended: but this one thing I do, forgetting those things which are behind, and reaching forth unto those

things which are before, I press toward the mark for the prize of the high calling of God in Christ Jesus."

When God has forgiven you, do not look back. Once he has forgiven you, move on to higher ground. He will not remind you again of those sins.

WISDOM THOUGHT

"Tomorrow's problems are unknown; they may cause new pain. Yesterday's are over with; some are still painful, but the pain is familiar--almost comfortable. Learn from the pain and move on."

CHAPTER NINE

SALVATION SCRIPTURES

Scriptures With Which You Should Become Familiar:

St. John 3:3: "Jesus answered and said unto him, Verily, verily, I say unto thee, Except a man be born again, he cannot see the kingdom of God."

II Corinthians 5:17: "Therefore if any man be in Christ, he is a new creature: old things are passed away; behold, all things are become new."

Romans 10:8-10: *"But what saith it? The word is nigh thee, even in thy mouth, and in thy heart: that is, the word of faith, which we preach; That if thou shalt confess with thy mouth the Lord Jesus, and shalt believe in thine heart that God hath raised him from the dead, thou shalt be saved. For with the heart man believeth unto righteousness; and with the mouth confession is made unto salvation."*

Romans 10:13: *"For whosoever shall call upon the name of the Lord shall be saved."*

Romans 5:1: *"Therefore being justified by faith, we have peace with God through our Lord Jesus Christ."*

I John 5:12: *"He that hath the Son hath life; and he that hath not the Son of God hath not life."*

I John 5:5: *"Who is he that overcometh the world, but he that* believeth that Jesus is the Son of God?"

I John 1:9: "*If we confess our sins, he is faithful and just to forgive us our sins, and to cleanse us from all unrighteousness.*"

John 3:15: "*That whosoever believeth in him should not perish, but have eternal life.*"

I John 5:1: "*Whosoever believeth that Jesus is the Christ is born of God: and every one that loveth him that begat loveth him also that is begotten of him.*"

Luke 13:3: "*I tell you, Nay: but, except ye repent, ye shall all likewise perish.*"

Acts 2:38: "*Then Peter said unto them, Repent, and be baptized every one of you in the name of Jesus Christ for the remission of sins, and ye shall receive the gift of the Holy Ghost.*"

Acts 4:12: *"Neither is there salvation in any other: for there is none other name under heaven given among men, whereby we must be saved."*

II Peter 3:9: *"The Lord is not slack concerning his promise, as some men count slackness; but is longsuffering to us-ward, not willing that any should perish, but that all should come to repentance."*

Romans 3:23: *"For all have sinned, and come short of the glory of God."*

Romans 5:7: *"For scarcely for a righteous man will one die: yet peradventure for a good man some would even dare to die."*

Ephesians 2:8: *"For by grace are ye saved through faith; and that not of yourselves: it is the gift of God"*

I John 5:14: *"And this is the confidence that we have in him, that, if we ask any thing according to his will, he heareth us."*

Luke 11:11: *"If a son shall ask bread of any of you that is a father, will he give him a stone? or if he ask a fish, will he for a fish give him a serpent?"*

SCRIPTURE FOR REDEDICATING ONES' LIFE AFTER BROKEN FELLOWSHIP

Many Christians fail to walk in victory because they are constantly plagued by memories of their past or they allow the enemy to convince them that God will not forgive their sins or falling short of what they have promised Him.

1 John 1:7-10:

"But if we walk in the light, as he is in the light, we have fellowship

59

one with another, and the blood of Jesus Christ his Son cleanseth us from all sin. If we say that we have no sin, we deceive ourselves, and the truth is not in us. If we confess our sins, he is faithful and just to forgive us our sins, and to cleanse us from all unrighteousness. If we say that we have not sinned, we make him a liar, and his word is not in us."

Memorize the scriptures that you have just read and always be prepared to give a ready answer. Remember that salvation comes only in the name of Jesus.

According to Acts 4:12:

"Neither is there salvation in any other: for there is none other name under heaven given among men, whereby we must be saved."

CHAPTER TEN

"TEAMWORK -- JESUS STYLE"

In the military, trained soldiers work together as they qualify per regulation. In doing so, they become team players. Their training consists not only in drill practice, but also under battle circumstances. The military provides uniforms as are provided for the Christian soldier.

Ephesians 6:11

> ***"Put on the whole armour of God, that ye may be able to stand against the wiles of the devil."***

We have to put on our uniforms spiritually. As a team, you should not allow division to show its head. We must remain united, so that we can win the lost with the power of the Holy Ghost.

Jesus Christ, the captain of our salvation, always gives His disciples' principles or ways to do things. To be successful, in winning the lost, we must recognize Jesus' ways or principles. Not only should we recognize them, but incorporate them in our life strategies.

For example, take Luke 10:1:

> ***"After these things the Lord appointed other seventy also, and sent them two and two before his face into every city and place, whither he himself would come."***

Note that Jesus appointed the seventy who would go out. They went out at His command. He sent them out into the hedges and highways to compel the lost back into His kingdom. Today, He has sent pastors and bishops out; but He also has sent lay members out. He has commissioned all, who believe, to go out and win souls for the glory of God.

Consolidate every one's involvement in soul winning; not just a few dedicated workers. This is the Lord's business. If we say that we love the Lord, we must be about His business. We need to get busy, as a team, working for the Lord.

Genesis 7:9 states:

> **"There went in two and two unto Noah into the ark, the male and the female, as God had commanded Noah."**

As we saw in Luke 10:1, the Lord sent them out "two by two". This meant that He intended for them to work as a team. *Teamwork* is very important in working for the Lord. He sent them out as two, so that they could share ideas and wisdom. It is the same for us. Going out in pairs means that we can share with one another, and assist when mistakes or misjudgments occur. It also means that we have a ready prayer partner as we witness. One must not underestimate the constant prayer covering of your partner. It is essential for any work of God.

We should rely upon *Teamwork* in every aspect, in the Ministry of Reconciliation. We should pray together, as a team, even before we go out. Then we decide which area to go to and which houses to visit, with the leadership of Jesus Christ.

In *Teamwork*, you learn to understand your partner. There should be one soul winner and one silent partner. The silent partner should be in agreement with the soul winner. He/she should be praying, and lifting up the soul winner and the people to whom the soul winner is witnessing.

In *Teamwork*, the soul winner will lead the discussion and give scriptures to the listeners. The scriptures should be specific to chapter and verse. The listeners should be able to read along and see it for themselves, so that they will know for sure that it is the genuine Word of God from the Holy Bible. The silent partner should assist the listeners with finding scriptures more quickly.

In *Teamwork*, both partners must be very patient with the lost candidates, and listen carefully and attentively to their problems. You must not judge them or be condemning in any way. You are there to show them the way out of their problems.

In *Teamwork*, the soul winner must be wise, mature, and very understanding. He should not act as if he knows everything, or that no one can tell him anything. He should both be humble and sensitive to the voice of God.

In *Teamwork*, the silent partner lifts the conversation in prayer, encourages the soul winner, and brings balance to the discussion when necessary. The silent partner should exhibit a meek and quiet spirit.

In *Teamwork*, the soul winner should not dominate the conversation, but give way for the silent partner to contribute. Give place to the partner to contribute to the conversation.

In Teamwork Jesus Style, there should always be the power of agreement.

Matthew 18:19-20:

> ***"Again I say unto you, That if two of you shall agree on earth as touching any thing that they shall ask, it shall be done for them of my Father which is in heaven. For where two or three are gathered together in my name, there am I in the midst of them."***

In Amos 3:3 we read:

> ***"Can two walk together, except they be agreed?"***

Where there is unity, there is strength. Both partners must constantly pray for one another. This will ensure that they can walk together in the agreement of God.

In life, you may think some things are insignificant; how minor or petty they are depends upon what end of the arrangement or contracts you are on. Regardless of how meager, get in agreement with your partner. You'll be glad you did.

66

Psalm 133:1:

> **"A Song of degrees of David.
> Behold, how good and how pleasant it
> is for brethren to dwell together in
> unity!"**

WISDOM THOUGHT

**"To a surgeon, in the midst of an operation, there is no
such thing as a small detail. Every slightest detail is a
matter of life and death."**

APPENDIX "A"

THINGS YOU SHOULD KNOW CONCERNING SOUL WINNING JESUS STYLE

WITNESSING TECHNIQUES

- Do not take a big Bible when going out; take a smaller less noticeable one.

- Rely completely upon the Holy Spirit to do the work for you.

- Remember to fast and pray the day prior to going out.

- Everyone needs salvation. It is our duty as born again, Spirit-filled believers to share Jesus Christ with everyone.

We must share Jesus with men, women, boys, and girls. **We must** share the gospel of Jesus with bill collectors, delivery people, lawyers, doctors, the learned, and the unlearned. There is no one who does not need to hear about Jesus.

68

A.　　People should say your home is a soul winning home.

B.　　Be a witness in words and deeds.

- Pray before going out.　Remember it is wise to go as Jesus told us in Luke 10:1 (two and two), it takes teamwork.

- Welcome people with love.　A "holy hug or handshake" will welcome them to their new life and walk with Jesus Christ.

- Explain to them that they need a covering, a Local Church.　Stress to them that they need a Local Church home that teaches the Word of God, according to the Bible.　Help them to understand that they need church leaders that truly live the Word of God.　This will help establish them in the faith of Jesus Christ.

- Admonish them to read their Bibles everyday, morning and evening. This is their spiritual food, and they must have it to grow. You can relate to them that they feed their bodies; now they must feed their spirit man.

- Share with them the importance of associating with strong Christian believers.

- Also mention to them the importance of not spending time alone with the opposite sex, if it is not their spouse.

- Stress that they must focus on living holy before the Lord.

APPENDIX "B"

THE "DON'TS" IN WITNESSING TO UNBELIEVERS

- Don't appear dirty, but appear decent. Remember, God looks upon the heart, but man looks upon the outward appearance.

- Don't go out with bad breath. Use mouth wash or mints. Don't let your breath keep someone from coming to Jesus Christ.

- Don't give out your home telephone number. Instead give them the church office number, or get their number. Check, with your church leaders, before giving out telephone numbers, verify them. You don't want to give out a non-working or an erroneous one.

- Don't become so spiritual that people cannot relate to you. Stay on a level that allows them to understand you, and relate to the Jesus that is within you.

71

- Don't act as if you are superior to them, or that you stand in judgment of them.

- Don't ask them to turn off their television. When allowed into their home, you should praise God you made it in. Speak quietly; they will have to turn it down or off.

- Don't speak in tongues. Normally people, whether unbelieving or irreligious, will not understand the concept of tongues; don't confuse them. If they show interest in being filled with the Holy Spirit; you can minister to them in that area when necessary. Let the Holy Spirit do the work.

- Don't cry with them after you have listened to their problems; be concerned and show that you care, but don't have a pity party with them.

- Don't be afraid or act fearful. Remember, "God has not given you a spirit of fear; but of power, love, and a sound mind."

- Don't speak loudly, but speak with love and boldness. "A soft answer turns away wrath."

- Don't attack your witness partner in the presence of your witness candidate.

- Don't try to witness to your loved ones who don't want to hear from you. Pray for them and live a holy life in their presence. God will send His soldiers to them.

"To succeed in life means that you have to step out of an ordinary line in life, and march to the sound of our creator, our Lord Jesus Christ."

WISDOM THOUGHT

"The trouble is that most of us have not learned to disentangle the notions of vulgar(crude) success and personal success. We constantly aim for goals that we think others will approve of; and we are pained to find that they have little to do with true happiness."

APPENDIX

And He gave some...for the work of the Ministry and for the Perfecting of the saints Ephesians 4:11-12

About The Authors

Their ministry is to those who are called of God-for ministry and individuals who consider themselves as a five-fold ministry gift; trained to know and walk in that gift. "A message for leaders and a message for the body", said the Lord

They were filled with the spirit in '78 and '80. Combined, they have sat under tutors and governors in the Word for almost 30 years in bible based teaching institutes. They remain connected to similar institutes of ministry training for continued ministry education.

As pastors and founders of BMWM, Inc., Success World Outreach Ministries--Church and School of Ministry, a school of Ambassadors and Champions for Christ, they spend many hours in personal training and enrichment. Their Success Evangelism Traveling Ministry has given them many opportunities to affect the lives of others. They are presently meeting in Raleigh, NC training Ephesians 4:11-12 ministry gifts in the Work of The Ministry.

Prior to opening the School of Ministry, they have traveled extensively to over ten states and in many cities. Their ministering has been to over 100 ministries churches, seminars and conferences. 'If you would like for them to minister in your place of ministry, write or give them a call.'

Under the Full Gospel Baptist Church Fellowship, Bishop Paul S. Morton being the First Presiding Bishop, Benjamin & Mercedes are serving as Directors of Evangelism for the State of North Carolina. This involvement covers over 50 churches in that state alone. God has called them to the Body of Christ, thank God for every opportunity to be a blessing to His people.

God has richly blessed their travels in the last 18 months. They have covered states from New York to Florida to Louisiana. Many leaders have invited them back several times because of the growth and maturity they are experiencing in their congregations. In some major cities they have been to different churches to the Glory of God. Many churches are now working together setting up mini-conferences, bringing them in for Christian Enrichment and Restoration Seminars.

Prior to attending CFC, their church involvement included missionary work, 1978-82 in Raleigh, NC, ministering in churches and on the streets and with college students, Rest Homes and at the Raleigh Rescue Mission and In-Home Bible Study Groups.

After attending Bible School under Dr. Timberlake, they worked with the Children's Ministry from 1982-1984, and as Deacon and Deaconess. In 1986 they became Teen Pastors--3 years, ministering the Word weekly to hundreds of teens, served on the Pastoral Staff at the end of 1988-89. There they served the senior pastors and worked as helps ministers with the Rest Home through the Home Cell Groups.

At the end of 1989 the couple was asked to "come aboard" as Associate Pastors on a full time weekly basis working at the ministry headquarters. They resigned their full time employment and fulfilled that call until 1994. The full time Staff Associate Pastors included two-three services on Sunday, Wednesday night, and working Monday through Friday providing Pastoral Care to the members and other administrative duties. This team served as Department Heads of the Outreach Ministries, including: Prison Ministry, Telephone Ministry, and Food & Clothing Distribution. They taught in the Christian School and were Area Coordinators for seven Home Cell Groups in different cities.

76

They served as Associate Pastors at Christian Faith Center, a church that has over 3000 members. Because of dedicated service in full time church ministry, they launched out into a full time traveling ministry with a letter of recommendation to over 80 pastors from their pastors, Dr. Mack & Brenda Timberlake, Jr. Going with the Spirit of the Lord, they have helped build up those and other ministries, imparting the prophetic anointing as well as soul winning techniques.

They have walked the streets in the city where the church is and personally won over 500 people(documented) to Christ in 1990, knocking on doors for nine months--twice a week 7-9 PM. Their pastor often said "if you want your church to grow, get this couple in your church and experience church growth".

God has invested a wealth of information and hands-on experience in these vessels and is making them available to mentor many in the Body of Christ. Receive them in the service of the Lord. After launching out in the Evangelistic Field, God confirmed what they have learned and experienced in the past 18 years. "Teach my people how to get set up and flow with me. Share with them, bring them to be one. Develop a base where they can come and be trained." He confirmed in their spirits and continues to expose them to so many things that will be of great assistance to the Body of Christ, you and His Ministry in your place.

Other Community Involvement

Pastors Benjamin & Mercedes Williams have served in many capacities in communities in Wake and Granville and Durham Counties, the State of North Carolina Prison Systems, the NC Council on Aging, the Occonechee Council Scouting Program. Among many other awards, she received the Distinguished Leadership Citation--one of North Carolina's highest volunteer awards. This couple has spent time ministering at noonday sessions at the Creedmoor Senior Center in Granville County. He has received volunteer awards from Granville county for his volunteer service with the Senior Citizens. She has served the nation as a member of the US Army & Reserve Component for seven years. They have many plaques and awards for their many hours of community service. This includes serving on the Board of the Resource Council of Triangle Institute. He obtained his B. S in Accounting at Shaw University in 1984 where he received recognition as a leader in religious services. He was nominated among the "Distinguished Young Men of America". She has been nominated among the "Distinguished Women of North Carolina".

They have ministered in many areas, rest homes in jails and prisons, on the streets and in churches, at crusades and in conferences. They have compassion for the lost.

TO GOD BE ALL PRAISE AND GLORY FOR THE THINGS HE HAS DONE.

Upcoming Books

The Ministry of Angels

Community Shakers

Mission Possible

The Glory

In His Image

See It Through His Eyes

Stop Running From The Prophetic Call

....

❏Pastor Williams, I am interested in attending the School of Ministry. Please send me the necessary information to get enrolled.

❏We are interested in your coming to our community, church to do a seminar or speak prophetically into our fellowship. I will be giving you a call. Send some information.

❏Please pray for me(us) for the following, _____

_____

_____

Soul Winning Jesus Style

For More Information Write:
**PO Box 19610
Raleigh, NC 27619**

Call today **1-919-528-1739**

or Leave a Message at the Message
Center at 1-919-685-8438

Pastors & Leaders Get SOUND

Prophetic Teaching that will **launch your ministry out** into
God's destiny for your life and ministry.
It will bring excitement to your walk with the Lord

Ask about *Christian Ministry Training*

World Outreach
Ministries

SUCCESS WORLD
OUTREACH
SCHOOL OF MINISTRY

b

ORDER FORM

NAME _____

ADDRESS _____

CITY _____

STATE, ZIP_____

QUANTITY _____

TOTAL DONATION(10.00 each) _____

FOR LARGE QUANTITIES CALL
1-919-528-1739

Make money orders and checks payable to: **Benjamin & Mercedes Williams.**

For Credit Card Orders: Enter your name as it appears on the card

---

Sign your name as it appears on the card

❑ M/C ❑ VISA

❑ Card Number_____

Expiration date _____

Please add an additional $2.00 for 1-15 books, $3.00--16-30, $4.00--31-45 books for postage and handling, call for larger quantities.

c